COME, HOLY SPIRIT

**A Service and Drama
for the Day of Pentecost**

NEVIN FEATHER
&
MYRTLE T. COLLINS

C.S.S. Publishing Company, Inc.
Lima, Ohio

COME, HOLY SPIRIT
A Service and Drama for the Day of Pentecost

6808 / ISBN 0-89536-790-4

Table of Contents

Material provided by Nevin Feather

Material provided by Myrtle T. Collins

Part I

Order of Service

"A Celebration of Pentecost"

A Celebration of Pentecost

Prelude

I. The Feast of Unleavened Bread

Narration by Pastor:

Pentecost — A strange word to us.

Pentecost — a word we never use except for one Sunday in the Christian church year.

Pentecost — what is the meaning of the word? What is its history? What purpose does it have for the lives of us modern Christians?

For the answers to our questions, we must return to the Jewish faith of our spiritual ancestors. The ancient Israelites of more than 2,500 years ago had some very important days of celebration which were an integral part of their religion. One of these special days was called the Feast of Unleavened Bread. Later on, the Passover meal would be incorporated into this feast. But the Feast of Unleavened Bread marked the start of the harvest season. It acknowledged God as the owner of the land — the source of all its products. In order to show their appreciation and thanksgiving for God's care by providing them with food, these Jews would bring the first cut sheaf of grain to the temple for sacrifice, and the sheaf of grain was waved before the altar. All the men who attended the ceremony danced an altar dance during which they sang the Hallel. The Hallel consists of the Psalms in our Bible that are numbered 113 to 118. As a small reenactment of the Feast of Unleavened Bread, let us sing a harvest hymn while the choir members come in carrying stalks of grain. I shall receive the grain from the choir members and bind the stalks into a sheaf and wave it before the altar. *(Place the sheaf in front of the altar when the hymn is finished.)*

A Harvest Hymn *(with the choir processing)* Suggestions: "Come, Ye Thankful People, Come" "Praise to God, Immortal Praise" "We Plow the Fields"

Narration:

Another portion of the Feast of Unleavened Bread was the presentation of two loaves of bread that had no leaven or yeast in them. The bread was made from the first harvested grain, but the people did not want to take the time for the leaven to work, so they made the bread without the leaven. They were in a hurry to get back to the harvest fields. This was the kind of bread that was made and eaten for the next seven weeks by all the devout Jews. We are indeed grateful for the Jewish friends in the community who made this unleavened bread for us. *(If there are no Jewish people in the area to do this, make your own unleavened bread. See the recipe in Part III.)* We now present the two loaves of unleavened bread and place them on the altar. *(Have two people from the congregation present the loaves to the pastor.)*

II. The Feast of Weeks

Narration:

The harvest season lasted for seven weeks — until the various kinds of grain were all reaped. Fifty days after the Feast of Unleavened Bread, the conclusion of the harvest season was celebrated with another festival called the Feast of Weeks. Seven weeks made forty-nine days, and the festival day added to the forty-nine made fifty days. In the Greek speaking world, for anything that had five parts or portions, or anything that indicated multiples of five, the prefix PENT was used. So the Feast of Weeks, which came on the fiftieth day after the Feast of Unleavened Bread, was also called Pentecost. To celebrate the Feast of Weeks or Pentecost, two loaves of bread were again brought to the altar, but this time it was leavened bread, bread with yeast, for now the harvest was over and there was time to wait for the leaven to make the bread dough rise. In celebration of the Feast of Weeks, also called Pentecost, we now present two loaves of leavened bread, and the *(Junior Choir)* will sing an anthem of praise that would be appropriate with this presentation of the leavened bread. *(Have someone in your own parish make two loaves of leavened bread and let them present the loaves to the pastor who, in turn, places the bread on the altar.)*

Anthem of Praise *(Sung by the choir(s), or a congregational hymn)*

III. Pentecost

Narration:

It was during the celebration of the Feast of Weeks, also called Pentecost, that the disciples of the resurrected Lord had gathered, much as we come here for worship and have a fellowship dinner afterwards. These disciples were talking over old times, recalling the days they had lived and worked with Jesus, but most of all recalling his crucifixion and resurrection. It was in this atmosphere, under these circumstances and conditions, that something strange happened to the disciples. Listen how it is described for us in the second chapter of the Acts of the Apostles. *(Read Acts 2:1-8, 12-14a, 22-24, 36-42.)*

Though the title of the senior choir's anthem is "The Gift of Love," the words of the last verse are quite appropriate for this occasion. "Come, spirit, come, our hearts control, our spirits long to be made whole. O come, spirit, come, Let inward love guide every deed. By this we worship and are freed. Amen."

Senior choir Anthem: "The Gift of Love" by Hal Hopson, Hope Publishing Company, Carol Stream, Illinois 60187. *(Another anthem may be substituted here, or a congregational hymn for Pentecost.)*

Presentation of the Pentecost banner

(A picture of the banner and directions for making it are enclosed.) The banner can be carried from the rear of the nave into the chancel while the senior choir sings their anthem or while the organist plays an appropriate hymn. The banner should be placed in the center of the chancel where most of the people can see it.

Children's Sermon *(This becomes an explanation of the symbolism of the banner. See Part II.)*

IV. Pentecost Today

Narration:

Thus we see how the Jewish Feast of Weeks, or Pentecost, was turned into a new kind of Christian celebration so that today, in our Christian churches, the day of Pentecost serves as a completely different purpose than its original association with the harvest. Continuing in this new vein of thought about Pentecost as a Christian celebration, we remember the account in the book of Acts records the events of that day concluded with baptism and the reception of new members into the Christian community.* We rejoice that we are able to have the same celebration in our church today. We have children to baptize and adults to receive as new members which we shall do now.

*If there is no one to be baptized or accepted as new members, conclude with this sentence: For centuries, many Christian churches have used Pentecost Sunday as a time to baptize people and to receive new members.

The service continues with Part V, the worship drama *The Treasure That Makes All Things New (see page 27).*

Part II
Children's Message

Children's Message

An explanation of the Pentecost banner

We are celebrating in our church today a special event that we call Pentecost. We've been telling the story of how this special day came into being over many years, and we've reached the point in telling the story where God's Holy Spirit came upon some of the disciples of Jesus and their friends in a very special way. This was not the first time that the disciples felt God's Spirit close to them, but some very strange and different things happened on this one occasion. So this day is remembered more than the others.

God's Holy Spirit seemed to be strongly present and wrapped itself around the disciples. God's Holy Spirit is represented by the symbol of a dove. Any time we see a picture or a wood carving of a descending dove, one that looks like it's flying with its head pointed down, it should remind us of the Spirit of God. Since God himself cannot be seen, in the Christian church we use the symbol of this dove to remind us of God. Look at the banner and see the descending dove with the nimbus, the circle around its head. When we see this symbol, we should always think about God's Spirit coming into our lives.

We see a circle made by arranging seven white doves. These seven doves represent the seven gifts of the Holy Spirit. The seven gifts are power, riches, wisdom, strength, honor, glory, and blessing. In the center of the circle we see two large capital S letters. These two S's are the initials for the two Latin words Sanctus Spiritus, which means, in English, Holy Spirit. (You may want to show the two Latin words printed out on paper.)

At the bottom of the banner we see something else. It is called a seven-tongued flame. It is a burning fire, like one over which we might roast hot dogs. Notice there are seven tongues of fire, like seven doves in the circle. This symbolism comes from the Bible, too. In the book of Acts where it describes the strange events of Pentecost, it tells about God's Holy Spirit coming over the disciples another way. It describes the Holy Spirit as tongues of fire resting over the disciples. So, we have this symbolism of the seven-tongued fire to remind us of God's Spirit.

Pentecost should be remembered as a happy day. It tells us that God is very real, that God is very close to us, and will help us, through his Spirit, any time we need him.

Part III
A Recipe for Unleavened Bread

A Recipe for Unleavened Bread

2 c. plain flour
1 ½ Tbsp. crisco
½ Tbsp. salt

Add milk to make good moist batter; if desired,
add 1 Tbsp. butter. Roll out dough into thin layer.
Cut in strips and prick with fork. Bake at 350
degrees until golden brown (about 10 to 15
minutes).

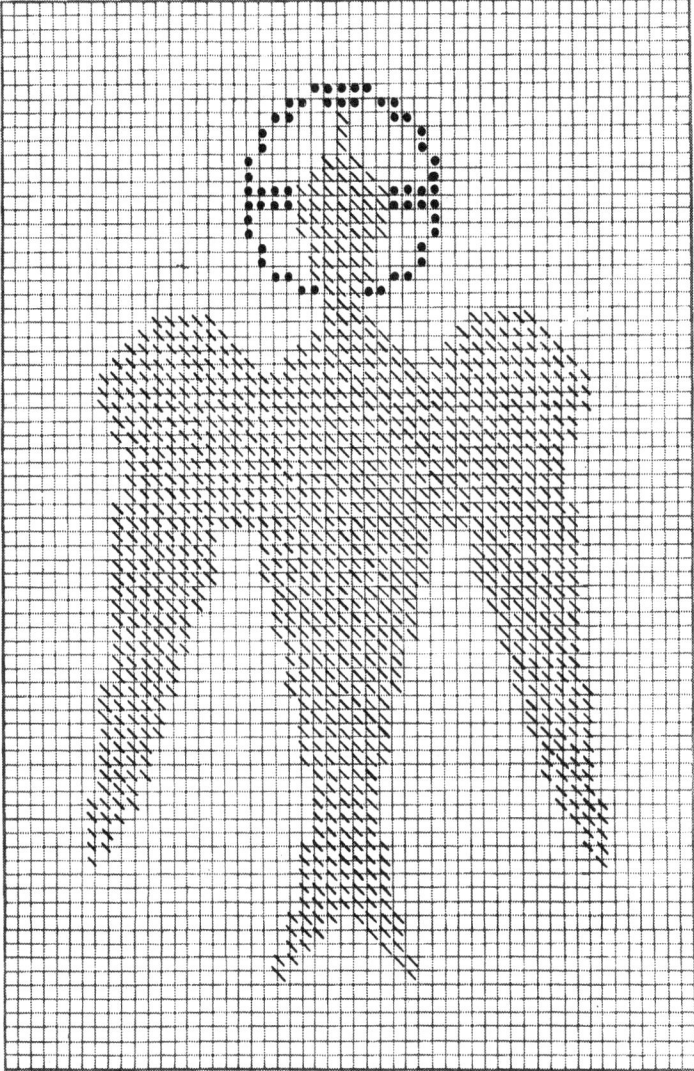

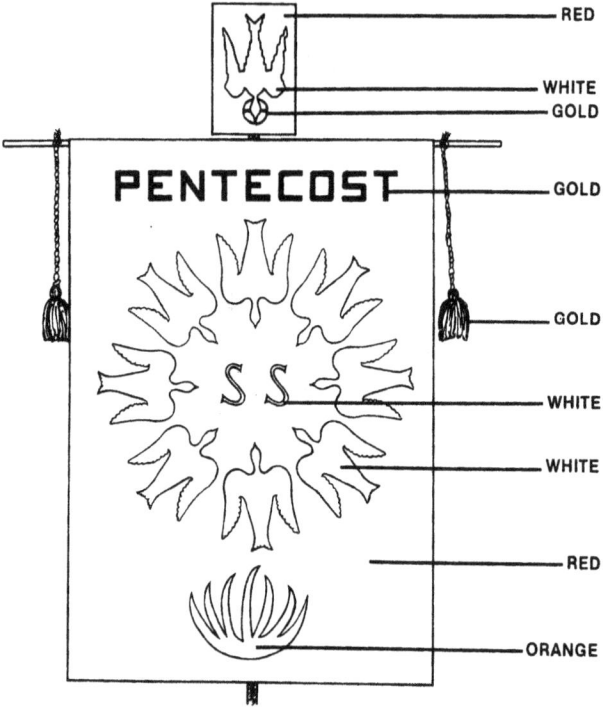

RED

WHITE
GOLD

PENTECOST

GOLD

GOLD

S S

WHITE

WHITE

RED

ORANGE

.

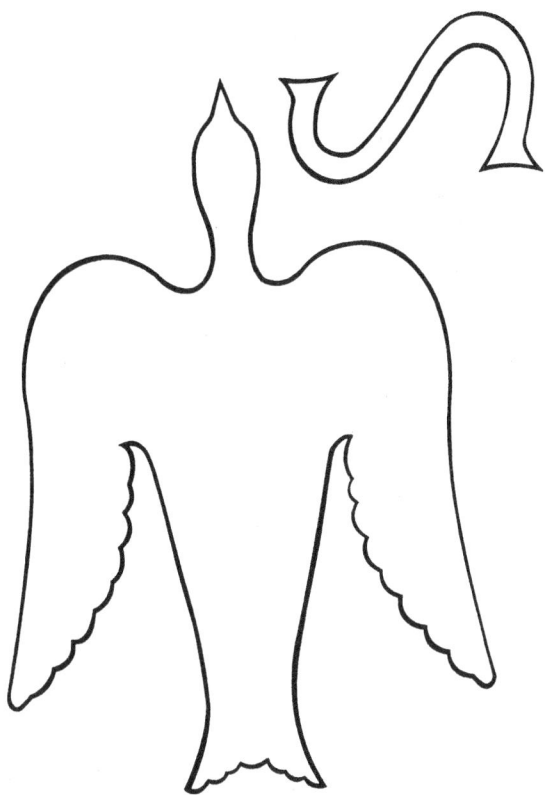

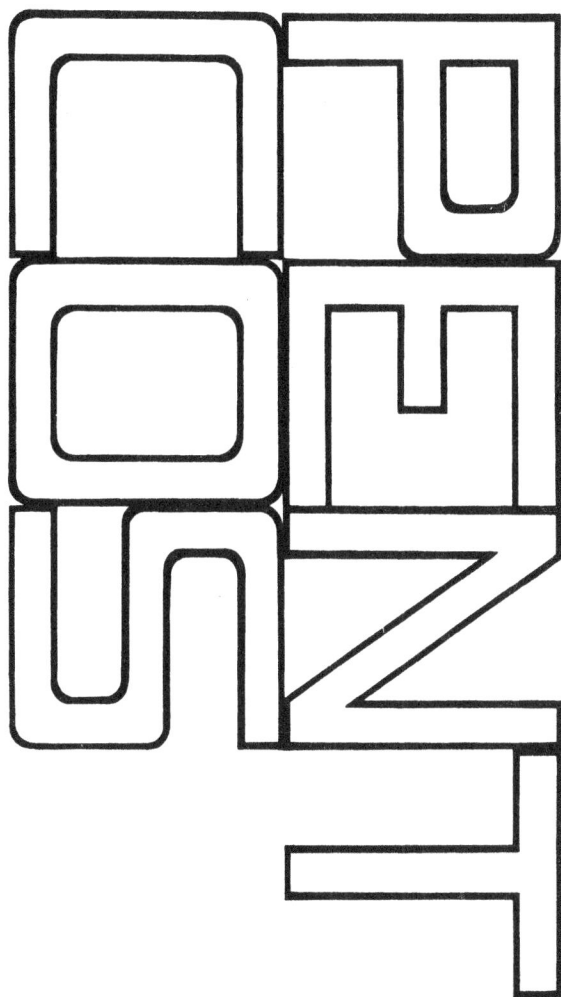

Part IV

Instructions for Making the Pentecost Banner

Instructions for making the Pentecost banner

Materials — red, white, gold, and orange felt

Enlarge pattern pieces to banner size you choose to make.
Cut letters for PENTECOST from gold felt.
Cut 7 doves and 2 S's from white felt.
Cut 1 seven-tongued flame from orange felt.
Arrange on red felt and fasten with glue.
Gold tassels may be added to the sides of the banner, or gold fringe
may be added to the bottom of the banner.

Optional

The smaller rectangle *(see picture)* with the descending dove and
nimbus is made from plastic canvas with a needlepoint stitch. It
is made with red, white, and gold 4-ply knitting yarn. The stitch-
ing pattern is on figure 4. Two of these are made and sewed
together with an overlapping stitch with a space left in the bottom center *(beneath the dove's head)* so the completed symbol can
be stripped down over the protruding pole on which the banner
is fastened.

Part V

Worship Drama

"The Treasure That Makes All Things New"

The Treasure That Makes All Things New

Cast of Characters:

The Visitor
Pastor A
Pastor B
Mother Church
Seven Children:
  Dick, whose interest is Public Relations
  John, whose interest is Outreach
  Cecil, whose interest is Parish Education
  Barbara, whose interest is caring Ministry
  Gerry, whose interest is Youth
  Margaret, whose interest is Worship & Music
  Virginia, whose interest is Stewardship
Verse Choir

Setting: The church on Pentecost Sunday

*(A **TALL STRANGER** saunters down the center aisle, looking around and into the faces of the congregation. He is dressed in everyday clothes, wearing a hat that is perched on his head in a cocky fashion. In time, he removes his hat and addresses the gathering.)*

VISITOR: Good morning! Hey, I hope you don't mind my being here. I'm an ordinary person with ordinary needs and I just walked in off the street.

How are you all? 's funny, isn't it, how a fella can walk by a building for years and never know what goes on inside. I live just down the way.

Well, I must say you look like a pretty decent lot. Clean — cleaner than I am; well dressed — better than I am.

Lots of kids here — I like that. You don't seem nearly as stuffy and stiff necked as I figured you might be. Hope you don't take offense at that . . .

(Looking around) Nice building this is — well kept. Pretty stained glass windows. Nice pews. You got a choir?

VOICE (from the choir loft — in melodic operatic style) Do we have a choir!

VISITOR: Ya got a Sunday school?

VOICE (from the congregation, about mid-section) Do we have a Sunday school!

(The VISITOR gets ready to pose another question when the two PASTORS appear from opposite sides of the chancel. They speak in unison.)

PASTOR and LAY ASSISTANT: I know it. I know it. I feel it coming. The next thing our visitor is going to ask is, 'Ya got a preacher?'

VISITOR: Well, you read my mind! And there you are — in your classic garb. Clean-cut chaps, I must say. (This to the audience) Ya got a sermon short and sweet — something not too heavy, not too syrupy, not too scary, just enough to give me a little lift and help me pass the time?

PASTOR: Shall we take him on, (insert L.A.'s name)? Shall we grant his wish?

L.A.: Sounds like a challenge, but how shall we do it? I hope the congregation understands that this is a little irregular.

PASTOR: Perhaps if we can get him to sit and listen for an hour he may get some answers to his interminable questions.

VISITOR: (defensively) Oh, no you don't — not one whole hour out of my Sunday morning. I've got things to do — gotta shop, get gas, play a little golf, wash my car. Ya see, I'm pretty busy and I only dropped in here because I had a few minutes to kill while they're fixing my Honda across the street. I didn't intend to stay — just kinda case the . . . place.

L.A.: Your Honda will be there in an hour.

PASTOR: It'll be there in two hours.

L.A.: Or three or four.

VISITOR: Hey! What are you two benign lookin' fellas tryin' to do — shanghai me into spending my precious Sunday in church?

PASTOR: Don't judge a book by its cover, friend. Stay!

VISITOR: Stay! *(indignantly)* You make me feel like a dog.

PASTOR: You said it. I didn't.

VISITOR: O.K. You've muzzled me. Let's get it over with. *(Sits)*

PASTOR: We've got him, *(insert L.A.'s name)*. Take it away!

L.A. goes to the pulpit. He is confused by the interruption and conveys this by wringing his hands, biting his lips, stroking his hair, and speaking very rapidly.

L.A.: Every congregation has goals — specific ones — and during the past several months we've been zeroing in on the needs of *(insert name of your congregation) (pause) (Then he repeats the same lines.)*

PASTOR *(noticing L.A.'s confusion, clears his throat as he approaches the pulpit) (name)*, I hate to interrupt you, but aren't you confused?

L.A.: What do you mean? You said 'Take it away'!

PASTOR: I know I did, but I meant 'Proceed with the liturgy.'

Things are getting out of hand.

L.A.: I couldn't agree more! *(to the congregation)* Let's sing a hymn while I calm my frazzled nerves. And won't you stand and greet one another before we sing the first four stanzas of "TAKE MY LIFE" *(or another appropriate hymn).*

L.A.: *(To the VISITOR)* Sir, won't you pay close attention now to the reading of the First Lesson by our verse choir.

VERSE CHOIR: *(seated in the second and third rows, rise, face the congregation, and read) (Director sits in the fourth row.)*

L.A.: *(to VISITOR)* Will you read with the congregation now the Second Lesson? *(Everyone reads, with L.A. leading.)*

(At the end of the Second Lesson the VISITOR rises as if to interrupt. L.A. politely ignores him and says quickly: The Gospel of the Day! *He or she reads it.)*

VISITOR: Don't I get a sermon? That *(fellow, woman)* there started one and you interrupted. So much for reading. Let's have some talking.

PASTOR: Patience, young man! I think I see where you are coming from. You are a likeable chap. Instead of a sermon as we usually think of it, let me share a story with you, complete with live characters. Now, mind you, this is an allegory. I think you might enjoy it. So make yourself comfortable.

VISITOR: *(Shakes head, then slowly sits down, resigned to witness the performance.)*

PASTOR: *(in pulpit)* Long, long ago, in a time that embraced every man, ancient and modern, lived a wise and wonderful mother. *(MOTHER appears from stage R, goes to lectern.)* Widowed at a young age, she reared the family in a God-fearing way. The day came, of course, when they scattered and had families of their own.

One day she sensed a special longing in her heart and sent messengers to gather the family together.

(CHILDREN enter) They all came in haste because they knew that whenever Mother beckoned she had a very good reason. For the sake of our story, let's call her Mother Church. The children, inspired by their sage and caring mother, had developed strong special interests. So it was that one day they all stood before her, and this is what she said to them:

MOTHER CHURCH:
> Children, good children, listen carefully. You are grown.
> From the nest you've long since flown.
> But you are still my children
> And our lives are intertwined.
>
> Remember, when you were small you'd try to find
> Treasures that were hid behind
> A chair, a sofa, or in a crack
> And try to be the first one back.

(The children nod affirmatively.)

> Now that you're grown, but children still,
> I've one request to make of you.
> Set out today to seek and find
> God's TREASURE THAT MAKES ALL THINGS NEW.
>
> Mount your Honda, ride your bike,
> Go by steed, or plane, or hike . . .
> Sail or swim, or even ski . . .
> Search and bring your finds to me!

(The children exit rapidly — two down each outer aisle and three down center.)

VERSE CHOIR: *(chanting rapidly)* She said,
> Mount your Honda, ride your bike,
> Go by steed, or plane or hike . . .
> Sail or swim, or even ski,
> Search and bring your finds to me!

MOTHER CHURCH: *(arms extended upward)*
Lord of life — see them go
Watch them, guide them, help them know
That the TREASURE they would find
Dwells within their hearts, their souls, their minds!

VERSE CHOIR: *(prayerfully)*
Lord of life — see them go
Watch them, guide them, help them know
That the TREASURE they would find
Dwells within their hearts, their souls, their minds!

(Here the soft roll of a drum is heard, barely heard — just enough to catch people's attention. It gradually fades away and PASTOR begins:)

PASTOR: *Days, weeks, months passed. Not one child returned. Restless and worried, the Mother blamed herself.*

MOTHER CHURCH:
> Dear God! I've failed to help them in their search. For this my own good name besmirch!

(She smites herself and turns aside.)

PASTOR: But the Great Mother's anguish turned to joy when she saw on the horizon the figures of all seven. Each was carrying a large box and each was wearing a broad smile. It was a joyous moment!

MOTHER CHURCH: *(elated, with arms outstretched)*
Children, children, each of you has brought a box
Holding treasure.
Have you the locks?
Let me hear what hides within,
_____, would you please begin?

P.R. Rep: Oh, Mother, I have here the gift of sharing the good news of our church — of generating a spirit of belonging. I really feel it is the treasure that makes all things new. You could call it Public Relations. Isn't that good, Mother?

34

MOTHER: It is good, indeed, _____. *(He turns away, dejected.)*

VERSE CHOIR: _____, she said it was good!

Outreach Rep: Good Mother, I searched long and hard and I bring here the gift of inviting others to worship with us and to witness Christ in the community.

New faces bring newness to our congregation. Surely you can't deny that that is the treasure that makes all things new. Isn't that good, Mother?

MOTHER: To be sure that is good, _____. *(He, too, turns away.)*

VERSE CHOIR: She said that was good, _____

Parish Ed. Rep: Fair Mother, I'm certain I have the treasure that you sent us to find. It is the ability to train our members in the study of God's Word to help us grow together.

Learning has to be the treasure that makes all things new. Isn't it, Mother? Isn't that good, Mother?

MOTHER: Of course, it's good, _____. *(He turns away, sad.)*

VERSE CHOIR: She said it was good, _____.

Caring Ministry Rep: Dear Mother, I do feel that my box contains the best of all the finds.

Inside is a tiny stone symbolizing caring for one another. Caring Ministry, you know. Things DO seem new when we become true ambassadors for Christ. Can you argue with that, gracious Mother?

MOTHER: It is difficult. You've done well, _____. *(She turns aside.)*

VERSE CHOIR: _____, she says you've done well.

Youth Rep: Proud Mother, who can top the treasure my box holds!

It is the hope of the church — the spirit of YOUTH! If anyone or anything can make all things new it is the lilt of laughter from happy young people! What do you say, Mother?

MOTHER: I say that's fine, _____. *(He turns away, saddened.)*

VERSE CHOIR: _____, she says that's fine.

Music Rep: My mother, the treasure I hold is surely THE one, for it is the very essence of worship and praise. What more can God want? What brings newness quicker than a glad heart with a glad song? Is there more to be found, Good Mother?

MOTHER: There is more, _____.

VERSE CHOIR: _____, she said there was more.

Stewardship Rep: *(very self assured)* Mother, I've listened to my brothers and sisters and they *did* bring priceless treasures, bless their hearts! Will they resent me if I produce the GREAT TREASURE THAT MAKES ALL THINGS NEW? I just know it's the willingness to share our God-given gifts, whatever they are — Good Stewardship! What do you say, Mother?

MOTHER: That, too, is good, _____. *(She turns away, sad.)*

VERSE CHOIR: _____, she said it was good!

PASTOR: The wise and wonderful Mother looked on her children with pity. Sorrow filled her being, for they had searched with diligence and their efforts were indeed commendable.

How deeply it hurt her to see their elation turn to dejection!

It was time to cheer them up.

MOTHER: Come, come, all you long faces! Look at me! I must assume some responsibility for your unhappiness. Perhaps I failed to prepare you well enough.

Let me review a story that you've all heard many, many times.

But, first a question, AND a clue: Do you remember that Pentecost comes fifty days after Easter?

CHILDREN: *(All nod affirmatively and look at each other, pleased.)*

MOTHER: We all know that human history is a record of man's inhumanity, hate, confusion — a picture of people trying to live without God.

We know that we must be in touch with God if this condition is to change. This isn't easily accomplished, however, because we erect walls of sin and guilt that keep us from receiving newness of life.

Isaiah said it so well: "But your iniquities have made a separation between you and your God and your sins have hidden his face from you so that he does not hear."

That's sad, isn't it? *(All nod)* The Good News is that God sent Jesus to reestablish contact between man and God. Remember that — *contact.*

When Jesus was on earth with his disciples, he promised them that, when it was time for him to leave, he would send the COM-FORTER — the HOLY SPIRIT — who would enter our hearts and enable us to carry on his work.

Dear children, it is no coincidence that you all returned to your home today! Today we celebrate the coming of the Holy Spirit to gather, to strengthen, and to guide us. Actually, this is the birthday of the Christian Church! *(The children smile!)*

Now let's discuss your precious discoveries. You have brought splen-did and important treasures. *But look at them!* They sit in isolation. Note the distances between them. Each is connected to *nothing.* Placed so, they will waste away, risk being kicked around.

CHILDREN: True, Mother, but what shall we do with them?

MOTHER: It's simple. Place each box close to another. *(They do.)* See, how they collectively build a unit? Can't you almost feel life generated by the closeness of each block? *(The boxes are placed to make a church. One child gets the cross and places it directly behind the edifice.)*

MOTHER: It is the Holy Spirit through whom God enters our hearts and lives IN us. He does that best when we work in concert with one another. Truly the greatest treasure that makes all things new is the Holy Spirit!

CHILDREN: *(prayerfully)*
Lord, we brought our treasures small
Each one thinking his was all,
But your SPIRIT took control,
Melded all into a whole.

*(The children then escort **MOTHER** to the front pew. All sit.)*

VERSE CHOIR: (all chant "Holy Spirit, Truth Divine," or another appropriate Pentecost hymn)

PASTOR: Let's all sing *ever so softly* this beautiful hymn — p. 257.

*(As the congregation completes the last line, **PASTOR** walks toward the **VISITOR**.)* So ends the story, my friend. You've been very attentive, very sober. May I ask why?

VISITOR: Sure — well, sure — I'll level with you. I came here to kill some time. I wanted to find sham and insincerity here, but something has happened to me while I've been sitting here.

An hour ago I would have said the Holy Spirit was a poet's dream, a preacher's fantasy . . . *(drifts off — looks away and starts to leave, then turns back)* Could I make a request?

PASTOR: Certainly.

VISITOR: Could we sing the last two verses of that hymn *Take My Life?* That really spoke to me, I mean *really* spoke to me. Could that be the Holy Spirit working in me already?

PASTOR: *(smiling)* Could be! Let's stand as we join our friend. Something tells me he's found the theme song for his life.

(Sing the remaining stanzas of "Take My Life".)

PASTOR: Now won't you join us in confessing the Apostles' Creed?

We will now receive the offering.

(The ushers come forward. The children could serve in this capacity.)

"On this day, O God, you taught the hearts of the faithful, sending them the Holy Spirit. On this day, too, you have brought us a Visitor who represents all seekers. May right judgment and the joy of the Comforter be ours, through Jesus Christ our Lord, who lives and reigns with you in the unity of the Holy Spirit, one God, forever. Amen."

*(The congregation sings Love Divine, All Loves Excelling. The acolytes go to the altar and extinguish the candles. The **MOTHER** rises, as do the seven children, and walks down the center aisle, smiling as she is escorted by her adoring children. The **VERSE CHOIR** exits the side aisle. The **PASTOR**, **LAY ASSISTANT**, and the **VISITOR** walk out together, smiling at one another.)*

ORGANIST: *(Plays the theme song, "Take My Life," until the pews are empty.)*

Appendix

Information About the Authors

NEVIN H. FEATHER is Pastor of Faith United Church of Christ, Hickory, North Carolina. A graduate of Franklin & Marshall College, Lancaster, Pennsylvania, and Lancaster (Pennsylvania) Theological Seminary, he has served congregations in Catawba County, North Carolina, and also at Landis, North Carolina. He and his wife, Cecil Mae, are the parents of three adult daughters.

MYRTLE T. COLLINS is an active member of Mount Calvary Lutheran Church of Colorado Springs, Colorado, where she participates in worship ministry through an active drama group within the congregation. "The Treasure That Makes All Things New" was originally created for use in her local congregation. A prolific writer, she has been published many times. A retired educator, she has had several articles on education published in a number of journals. Published book titles include *Teaching English to Brazilian Children, Survival Kit for Teachers (and Parents), You are Somebody Special,* and *Families Walking Together.* She and her husband, DWane, live in Manitou Springs, Colorado.

www.ingramcontent.com/pod-product-compliance
Lightning Source LLC
Chambersburg PA
CBHW071759020426
42331CB00008B/2320